A Special Edition for Friends of

PLANT CONSTRUCTION COMPANY, L. P.

California's development over almost two centuries has depended in large measure on the state's natural resources. In the nineteenth century mining, agriculture, and lumbering were keys to economic growth that transformed California from a remote outpost on the Pacific Coast to a vigorous economic giant. Charles Richard Miller was one of the young photographers who came west to document that expansion, in particular the logging and railroading activities in Siskiyou County. Arriving around 1900, he found in Mt. Shasta a place of spectacular beauty and natural assets that had attracted San Francisco's legendary entrepreneurs such as William Randolph Hearst and naturalists and artists such as John Muir and William Keith. *Mt. Shasta Camera* demonstrates Miller's keen observation of the world around him illuminated through his photographs.

Have a healthy, happy and prosperous New Year!
January 2005

Mossbrae Falls near Shasta Springs, ca.1906

MT. SHASTA CAMERA

Baldwin locomotives No.10 and No.8 of the McCloud River Railroad at the summit between McCloud and Upton, ca.1905.

MT. SHASTA CAMERA
THE PHOTOGRAPHS OF CHARLES RICHARD MILLER

WAYNE BONNETT

WINDGATE PRESS
SAUSALITO :: CALIFORNIA

Mt. Shasta from Grass Lake, ca.1906, by Charles R. Miller.

CONTENTS

FIRST EDITION

Printed in Korea by Sung In Printing America
ISBN 0915269-16-3
Windgate Press, P.O. Box 1715, Sausalito, California 94966
www.windgatepress.com

Rolling logs at the base of Mt. Shasta, McCloud River Lumber Company, ca.1905.

INTRODUCTION

Charles Richard Miller was one of the rugged and adventurous photographers who moved across the western states a century ago wherever opportunity and challenge led them. Born in Iowa in 1875, Miller moved west to Portland, Oregon as a young man and took up the dry-plate view camera as a means of livelihood. Around 1898 he began taking pictures in the Mt. Shasta region of Northern California, in particular the logging camps and lumber mills. Quite likely he associated himself with druggist LeRoy Lee in Sisson where, in 1900, Lee advertised for sale "photographs of the highest quality." Between 1905 and 1908, Charles Miller lived in the company mill town of McCloud at the base of Mt. Shasta and maintained a photographic studio there. During that time he did his finest work, both for the McCloud River Railroad and its parent, the McCloud River Lumber Company. In addition, Miller worked on commission in 1906 for the Lamoine Lumber and Trading Company and, in 1908, for the Northern California Lumber Company in Hilt.

Of the many hundreds, perhaps thousands, of photographs Miller made around Mt. Shasta and in McCloud, fewer than two hundred survive. They show Miller to be a skilled artist and craftsman capable of creating astute as well as aesthetically superb documentary photographs. He was comfortable in the world he photographed. An outdoors man capable of climbing Mt. Shasta and roughing it in the woods, Miller was at ease around loggers, mill workers, and railroad men. He mixed well with the wealthy too, the industrialists, bankers, and capitalists such as William Randolph Hearst who frequented the McCloud River basin in pursuit of trout and other rustic pleasures. From what little is known of Miller's personal life, he appeared sociable, loved the outdoors, worked hard, enjoyed family life and the company of both men and women.

The magnet that drew Charles Miller and other photographers to Mt. Shasta, aside from the dormant volcano's breath-taking beauty, was economic optimism generated by the railroad. The same sense of opportunity brought big money investors from San Francisco to Mt. Shasta. The Southern Pacific Railroad promoted its new Shasta Route, the *Road of a Thousand Wonders*, enticing visitors to partake of the local springs along the main line and the excellent hunting and fishing of the McCloud River region. Industrialists also saw great promise in the relatively untouched pine and fir forests that stretched for miles around the base of the mountain. The railroad that brought about such promise had been a long time coming.

The economic advantages of linking Oregon to California by rail were obvious even before completion of the transcontinental railroad in 1869. A route from Marysville, California to Portland, Oregon was surveyed as early as 1864. Then as now, the steep canyons of the upper Sacramento River and the Siskiyou Mountains near the California-Oregon border presented physical barriers that restricted travel between the two states. Early trappers and explorers had discovered natural passes through the mountains. Now the challenge was to drive steel rails through that rugged country, a feat comparable to spanning the high Sierra. Competing companies began working southward from Portland on the Columbia River and northward from Sacramento. By 1872 rails north had reached the town site of Redding and progress stalled there, extending only forty miles over the next decade. In Oregon, the rails reached south to Ashland by the mid-1880s. Travel was accomplished over the 126 miles between those two points by a twenty-four-hour stage coach journey. After several more years of difficult grading, tunneling, trestle building, and track laying, the last spike connecting California to Oregon was driven at Ashland, Oregon, December 16, 1887. The various railroads that had struggled across the mountains under control of the Central Pacific Railroad, now consolidated as Southern Pacific's Shasta Division, stretching from Redding in the south to Ashland in the north.

The new rails up the Sacramento River canyon between the Trinity and Cascade Mountains and across the Siskiyous presented to the traveler both marvelous and terrifying sights. Passenger trains crossed wide chasms on tall wooden trestles vibrating under the load, crawled through long tunnels filled with asphyxiating smoke, and careened along tight curves clinging to precipitous canyon walls. To counter the visual perils, Southern Pacific promoted through its literature the scenic wonders of the region, gushing springs and spectacular forests. Mt. Shasta, gleaming under its eternal glacial cap, cast its shadow over some of the grandest scenery in America, all viewed from the comfort of a Pullman car.

As expected, the completed railroad brought new economic life to the region. While tourists saw the mountain grandeur and drank the salubrious waters of local springs, lumbermen saw trees at long last within reach of major markets. Logging railroads, spurred off the Southern Pacific main line, transformed existing logging camps near the base of Mt. Shasta. Sawmills could reach deeper into the woods, and logs could be loaded on railroad flatcars rather than hauled by oxen to the sawmills.

Photographers had recorded the railroad's progress at every step. Southern Pacific employed its own cameramen while free-lance photographers roamed the Siskiyou and Trinity Mountains capturing breathtaking images of Mt. Shasta, the McCloud, Pitt, and Sacramento Rivers for a growing market in scenic photos. By 1900 postcard views of the region had circulated in the East, attracting even more tourists.

Charles Miller, twenty seven years old in 1902, moved down from Portland to Mt. Shasta that year, casting his lot with other opportunistic photographers. He settled in Sisson, a logical choice, since that town was growing rapidly and was on the main line of the Southern Pacific Railroad. Miller pitched his tent on a vacant lot below the freight depot and began to look for more permanent lodgings. In a few months, his wife and their young son arrived in Sisson from Portland. He may have returned to Portland or tried to keep studios both there and in Sisson. His Portland studio was listed in the 1901-02 Portland business directory. Within a few years Miller advertised his photographic studio, located in the Requa Building in Sisson, the same building as Lee's drug store.

Charles Miller, far right, atop Mt. Shasta in 1903.

Miller's bread-and-butter photographs in those days were views of Mt. Shasta in its various moods, which he could sell to passing railroad travelers. Few mountains in North America are as dramatic to behold from any viewpoint in any season. Miller often traversed the slopes of the mountain with his camera, winter and summer, and climbed adjacent peaks to gain vantage points. That summer of 1902 Miller, along with seven other local men, climbed to the summit of Mt. Shasta. He took his camera along and, according to the *Sisson Mirror,* "procured many handsome photographs." Miller became an enthusiastic climber and the following summer he ascended the mountain again, this time as leader of a party of climbers. Most climbers of Mt. Shasta, including Miller's party, started out from Sisson by horse, up twelve miles to the timber line at Horse Camp. After an overnight rest, they started just before sunrise on the eight-hour hike up the almost 45-degree angle of the southern face of the volcano, pausing at Thumb Rock before advancing on the summit. A journalist in Miller's party, George Hamlin Fitch of San Francisco, kept an account of the climb and later published it in the October 1903 issue of *Sunset Magazine*. In addition to their climbing and camping gear, Miller carried his 8 by 10-inch view camera and glass dry plates to record the event in photographs. From the heights of Mt. Shasta, Miller could look down on McCloud with its booming sawmill and the logging railroad that skirted the base of the mountain all the way to Upton.

Miller soon took his camera to McCloud and found opportunity there. The McCloud Lumber Company, shipping over 400,000 board feet of lumber daily, was the largest logging operation in the region. The Company commissioned Miller to record logging operations as well as activities in the town and it's sawmill. His work for the Company led him back and forth between Sisson and McCloud, a twelve-mile journey on the McCloud River Railroad. The trips became so frequent that Miller decided to relocate to McCloud, perhaps prompted by the Company's offer of a house for his studio in the heart of town. By October, 1905, he had sold his interest in the picture business in Sisson and relocated his business and family to California Street in McCloud. He may have sold many of his early glass negatives and his business to Jervie Henry Eastman, a competitor in in Sisson who went on to become one of California's most prolific photo postcard publishers. Some of Miller's early photos appear under the Eastman imprint in the 1920s.

After 1905 Miller continued to travel with his camera. In early May 1906, for example, Miller took the train to San Francisco to photograph the earthquake and fire aftermath. He returned with dramatic views of the burned district and put them on sale at his studio. To promote his scenic views, Miller traveled also to Portland, Klamath Falls, San Francisco and, no doubt, towns and cities in between, wherever he might find a market for his work.

Miller enjoyed regional recognition as a photographer and found plenty to keep him busy. He produced promotional photo postcards for the McCloud River Lumber Company and recorded each new facility and expansion. Also he traveled through northern and western Siskiyou County accompanied by Secretary Nolton of the county chamber of commerce, taking scenic advertising views. He continued to operate out of McCloud and photograph the progress of the McCloud Lumber Company and the McCloud River Railroad as that line extended its tracks east. By 1908 Miller decided he had run his course in the Mt. Shasta area. In early 1909 he moved his studio to Klamath Falls, Oregon, one hundred miles northeast of McCloud. Exactly what triggered his move is unrecorded, but one can assume his main motivation was economic. The Southern Pacific completed its long-awaited rail extension into Klamath Falls that year and logging in the region was poised for rapid expansion.

Miller quickly became established on Main Street in Klamath Falls, visiting Sisson and McCloud occasionally as business required. The *Sisson Headlight* reported in May, 1909, that Miller was in town with some "pretty views" of Siskiyou County, "finished up in colors. Charley has been taking some views in Scott Valley lately and a lot of his work will go to the [Alaska-Yukon-Pacific] Exposition at Seattle this summer."

In Klamath Falls, Miller formed the Miller Post Card Company, also known as the Miller Photo Company. He published a variety of real photo postcards with those imprints including many views of hunting and fishing, and rodeo cowboys. He continued to take postcard views of McCloud and other locations in Siskiyou County. In 1913 Miller was granted along with the Kiser Photo Company of Portland a license for photographic privileges at Oregon's Crater Lake National Park. Kiser's license was not renewed in 1915, leaving Miller with the exclusive right to photograph Crater Lake scenery and sell postcards there. That same year Miller bought out his Klamath Falls associate Glen Johnson.

As time passed, Miller's interests and changing times led him to activities besides photography. People were beginning to travel by automobile. Simple, affordable Kodak cameras plus the automobile meant ordinary people, his customers, could travel and take pictures of their own. New visual distractions competed with souvenir photos for the public's attention. Movies came to Klamath Falls' Orpheus Theatre around 1910. In 1915 fire gutted the building. Insurance covered only half the cost of reconstruction and the Orpheus languished into 1916. Miller stepped in, took over the lease and the management as well. He contracted for movies, vaudeville acts, and musical programs. Miller ran the business for about two years before turning over the lease to a man from Sisson.

Life changed for Charles Miller in the 1920s. After 1922 Miller and his Miller Photo Company were no longer listed in the Klamath Falls phone directory or business directory. Perhaps it was the nation-wide influenza epidemic of 1918 which struck hard at Klamath Falls. Perhaps his photo business was declining, or maybe his interests led him in other directions. What little is recorded of those years could be an explanation. In 1921 his fifteen-year-old son, Arthur Bliss Miller, died. His postcards printed

Charles Miller trout fishing in the McCloud River, ca.1905.

in the mid-1920s were no longer stamped "Miller Photo Company," but "Underwood Pharmacy, Kodak Department, Klamath Falls, Oregon." Then, in 1925, Charles R. Miller emerged in Klamath Falls as manager of the White Pine Molding Company. He continued in that capacity until his death and burial in 1934 in Linkville Cemetery, Klamath Falls.

Miller's photo postcards circulated for decades and today are sought after by collectors. His original photographs and albums found their way over time into private collections, museums and libraries. These surviving photographs, though relatively few, are Charles Miller's legacy. They speak eloquently of the logging camps and railroads around Mt. Shasta in a moment of history.

A SAMPLE OF THE McCLOUD RIVER TROUT FISHING.

Miller PHOTO.

Charles Miller's postcard views reveal his keen interest in hunting and fishing in the river basins beneath 14,161-foot Mt. Shasta. Long before Miller and his countrymen, the region had been home and hunting grounds to the Wintu and Okwanuchu tribes, who lived in small villages between the McCloud River and the Upper Sacramento River. Beginning in the 1850s, Americans and Europeans came, including naturalists John Muir and Joaquin Miller who vividly described the region. The lush country inspired artists William Keith and Thomas Hill, whose popular paintings helped spread the word about this sportsman's paradise.

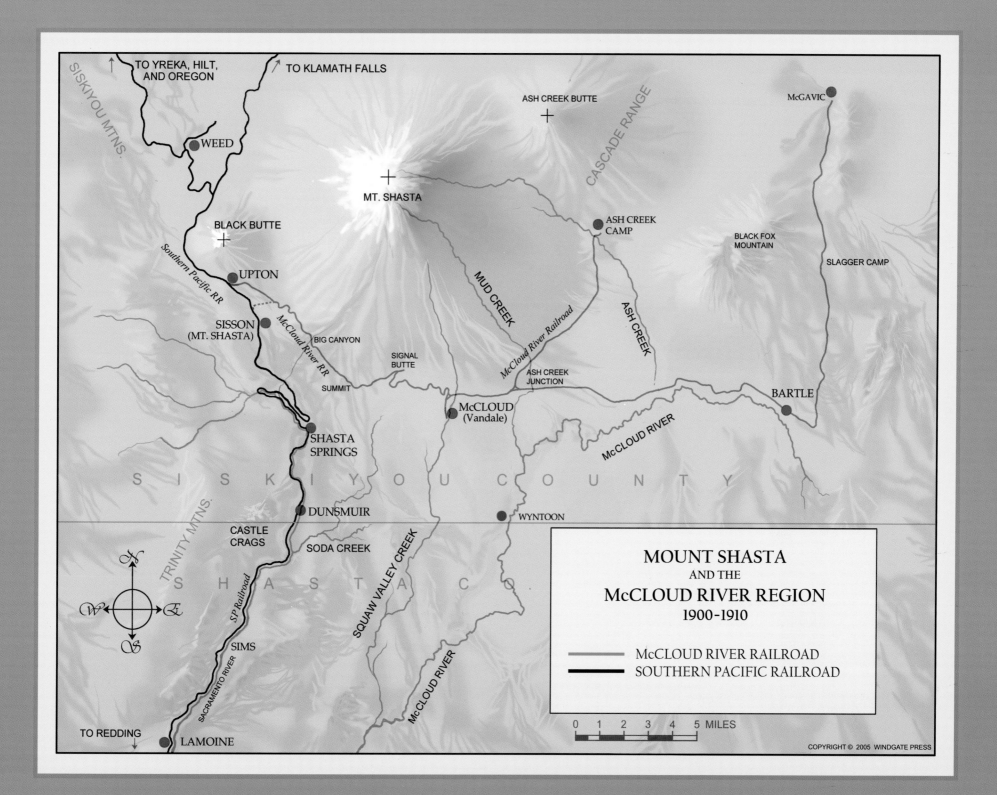

TO YREKA, HILT, AND OREGON

TO KLAMATH FALLS

SISKIYOU MTNS.

WEED

ASH CREEK BUTTE

CASCADE RANGE

McGAVIC

MT. SHASTA

BLACK BUTTE

ASH CREEK CAMP

BLACK FOX MOUNTAIN

SLAGGER CAMP

Southern Pacific RR

UPTON

MUD CREEK

SISSON (MT. SHASTA)

McCloud River RR

BIG CANYON

McCloud River Railroad

ASH CREEK

SIGNAL BUTTE

SUMMIT

ASH CREEK JUNCTION

BARTLE

McCLOUD (Vandale)

SHASTA SPRINGS

McCLOUD RIVER

SISKIYOU COUNTY

DUNSMUIR

WYNTOON

CASTLE CRAGS

TRINITY MTNS.

SODA CREEK

SQUAW VALLEY CREEK

SHASTA CO.

SP Railroad

N
W E
S

McCLOUD RIVER

SIMS

Sacramento River

TO REDDING

LAMOINE

MOUNT SHASTA
AND THE
McCLOUD RIVER REGION
1900-1910

—— McCLOUD RIVER RAILROAD
—— SOUTHERN PACIFIC RAILROAD

0 1 2 3 4 5 MILES

Big wheels near Ash Creek Camp, McCloud River Lumber Company, ca.1907.

A PORTFOLIO

C. R. Miller

Middle Falls of the McCloud River, ca.1910.

Mt. Shasta from McCloud, ca.1906.

Locomotive No.5 and flatcars with yellow pine logs, McCloud River Railroad, ca.1901.

Sixteen horses and mules pulling logs, probably Coggins Brothers Lumber Company south of Weed, ca.1906.

Original Scott and Van Arsdale sawmill and pond at McCloud, ca.1904.

The town of McCloud from atop the sawmill, ca.1904.

Drained millpond with pine logs, McCloud River Lumber Company, ca.1906.

Sawmill interior with log carriage and band saw, McCloud, ca.1907.

Sawmill workers, McCloud River Lumber Company, ca.1907.

Loggers at Elk Creek camp, McCloud River Lumber Company, ca.1904.

Big wheels used to drag logs to railroad landing in the woods, McCloud River Lumber Company, ca.1905.

Big wheels at Camp No.4, McCloud River Lumber Company, ca.1906.

Dragging a massive yellow pine log with horses, McCloud Lumber Company, ca.1903.

Dragging a yellow pine log with steam tractor, McCloud River Lumber Company, ca.1904.

Dolbeer steam donkey with vertical capstan, Northern California Lumber Company, 1908.

Bull donkey with horizontal capstan, Lamoine Lumber & Trading Company, 1906.

Log chute bridging steep ravine with cribbing, Northern California Lumber Company, 1908.

The same chute, one and one-half miles long, crossing ravine, 1908.

Steam yarding donkey near Hilt, Northern California Lumber Company, 1908.

Yarding logs from chute with steam donkeys, Northern California Lumber Company, 1908.

Track-laying crew and flatcars loaded with steel rails and wooden ties, McCloud River Railroad, ca.1907.

Portable camp cabins on flatcars, McCloud River Railroad, ca.1907.

Logging Camp No.1, McCloud River Lumber Company, ca.1905.

Loggers at rest, Camp No.1, McCloud River Lumber Company, ca.1906.

Meal time at a logging camp, McCloud River Lumber Company, ca.1907.

Mess tent at a logging camp, McCloud River Lumber Company, ca.1905.

Parbuckling logs onto flatcars with bull donkey, Ash Creek Camp, McCloud River Lumber Company, ca.1905.

Another view of parbuckling logs, Ash Creek Camp, McCloud River Lumber Company, ca.1905.

Best steam tractor and four-wheeled log wagon, McCloud River Lumber Company, ca.1910.

McGiffert log loader with stationary boom and flatcars, Northern California Lumber Company, 1908.

43

Locomotive No.15 near Black Fox Mountain, McCloud River Railroad, ca.1907.

44

Locomotive No.14 or 15 on the trestle east of Bartle, McCloud River Railroad, ca.1908.

Loading logs on flatcar, Lamoine Lumber & Trading Company, 1906.

46

Trestle at Slate Creek, locomotives No.1 and No.2, Lamoine Lumber & Trading Company, 1906.

Shasta Springs bottling works, depot, and spring house, ca.1902.

Southern Pacific rotary snow plow clearing tracks at Shasta Springs, ca.1903.

Southern Pacific passenger train crossing Big Canyon trestle between Cantara and Mott, ca.1910.

Wedge snow plow, McCloud River Railroad locomotives No.11 and No.12, at Sisson, ca.1905.

Wedge snow plow and five locomotives clearing tracks, McCloud River Railroad, January 1914.

Southern Pacific rotary pushing into McCloud, January 1914.

Sawmill on Cottonwood Creek near Hilt, Northern California Lumber Company, 1908.

Log dump and millpond at Cottonwood Creek mill, Northern California Lumber Company, 1908.

Original Scott and Van Arsdale sawmill at McCloud, Mt. Shasta in background, ca.1908.

McCloud from atop sawmill with new mill in background, ca.1908.

Building millpond for new sawmill at Squaw Valley Creek on the north side of McCloud, ca.1905.

Completed millpond for new sawmill, McCloud, ca.1907.

Powerhouse, box factory, and planning mill. McCloud River Lumber Company, ca.1908.

Ash Creek sawmill, McCloud River Lumber Company, ca.1902.

Sawmill workers, McCloud River Lumber Company, ca.1908.

McCloud school, ca.1908.

Thirty-inch-wide pine planks, Northern California Lumber Company, 1908.

Log on carriage with bandsaw, Cottonwood Creek mill, Northern California Lumber Company, 1908.

Buckers at rest with pine logs, McCloud River Lumber Company, ca.1908.

McCloud River Railroad crew with combination passenger and mail car, ca.1907.

Lawndale, with executive houses near depot, McCLoud, ca.1906.

Locomotive No.12 (ex-No.1) at McCloud depot, ca.1908.

Locomotive No.9 at Big Canyon fill, McCloud River Railroad, ca.1904.

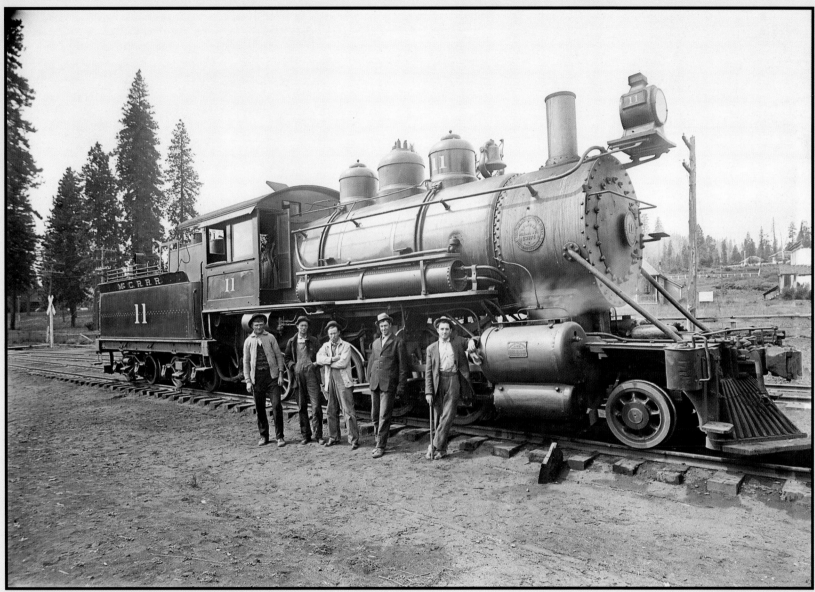

Locomotive No.11 near McCloud depot, McCloud River Railroad, ca.1904.

Climax locomotive of the Northern California Lumber Company with log flats, 1908.

Private car of President J. H. Queal, McCloud River Lumber Company, ca.1907.

Locomotive No. 7 and dormitory cars, Camp No.4, McCloud River Railroad, 1914.

Locomotive No.12 ready for daily passenger run to Upton from McCloud, ca.1906.

McCloud depot with Hotel McCloud in background, ca.1908.

Hotel McCloud, ca.1908.

Vauclain compound locomotive No.6 with flatcars and fir logs, McCloud River Railroad, ca.1904.

Logger with fir log, Northern California Lumber Company, 1908.

Portraits taken in Miller's studio, McCloud, ca.1906.

80

Portraits taken in the woods, water boy, above, and fallers, right, ca.1905.

Bartle, east of McCloud, McCloud River Railroad, ca.1908.

Depot at Bartle Station, McCloud River Railroad, ca.1908.

Lamoine, on the Southern Pacific Shasta Line, summer 1906.

Climax No.1, and Shay No.2, Lamoine Lumber & Trading Company narrow gauge railroad, 1906.

Sanford Pass switchbacks, Lamoine Lumber & Trading Company railroad, ca.1912.

Logging camp No.2, Lamoine Lumber & Trading Company, ca.1912.

Oldsmobile track inspection engine, Lamoine Lumber & Trading Company, 1906.

Southern Pacific log train derailed on Ash Creek branch, McCloud River Railroad, 1900.

Compound double locomotive No.6 derailed, McCloud River Railroad, ca.1902.

Log train derailed north of Bartle, McCloud River Railroad, ca.1905.

Southern Pacific flatcars with wood racks derailed, McCloud River Railroad, ca.1908.

Locomotive No.5 derailed, McCloud River Railroad, ca.1905.

Auto road from Castle Crags to McCloud, ca.1908.

Toll road in Soda Creek Tract, Northern California Lumber Company, 1908.

96

McCloud River, Burns and Waterhouse residence in the distance, ca.1905.

Burns and Waterhouse residence on the McCloud River near Wyntoon, ca.1905.

Wyntoon castle of Phoebe Apperson Hearst under construction, ca.1903.

Wyntoon completed in 1905, designed by Bernard Maybeck.

Big Springs on the McCloud River, ca.1908.

Black Butte and Mt. Shasta, ca.1904.

PORTFOLIO NOTES:

14. Middle Falls of the McCloud River. Miller came to know the river well, combining his love of fishing and photography. Widely circulated photos like this, taken around 1910, drew visitors to the river.

15. The town of McCloud, close by Mt. Shasta with unobstructed vistas of the mountain, made an excellent setting for post card views. Miller could, and often did, stand in the middle of a street and capture a scene such as this.

16. McCloud River Railroad locomotive No.5 pulling yellow pine logs to the sawmill sometime after 1900. This engine had a tendency to come off the rails. It began its career at McCloud as half of an odd combination of two identical locomotives joined back to back, an attempt by Baldwin Locomotive Works to provide power with flexibility for tight curves on logging railroads. (See Page 90)

17. Sixteen horses and mules pulling log wagons make a clear contrast to the previous picture of a log train pulled by a locomotive. This circa 1906 photo was often cropped by others to eliminate the steam tractor at the far right, making it appear the scene was earlier than 1900. In Miller's time around Mt. Shasta, the logging industry was phasing out animal power in favor of steam power, although horses remained in service until the mid-1920s.

18. The first sawmill built by Scott and Van Arsdale, owners of the McCloud River Lumber Company, was on the site of the old Friday George mill. Miller managed to make a rather prosaic scene into an aesthetically pleasing one by his use of reflections. This mill used two circular saws mounted one above the other to cut logs into lumber. When a larger bandsaw mill was built in McCloud, this mill was renamed No. 2.

19. McCloud from atop the sawmill, log pond in the foreground. Miller, always eager for the shot, climbed to the rooftop with his bulky camera. The large building at left rear is the Company Store, left foreground is a Chinese cook house, and on the right are workers houses.

20. The log pond, apparently drained, with a big supply of pine logs. Logs were hauled up the chute at right rear to the saw by an endless chain studded with steel hooks.

21. Inside the mill, the setters manipulated the log on a moving carriage by a system of levers and dogs that turned and positioned the log for the right cut. After each pass through the continuously moving saw blade, the carriage moved back and the log was shifted the desired distance for the next pass. The bandsaw blade, rising vertically, can be seen at right.

22. Sawmill workers at McCloud. Each shift consisted of men with specific jobs and representing several nationalities. In Miller's time at McCloud, more than half the workers were Italian, some Greek and Scandinavian. The workers lived in town in houses provided by the Company.

23. The Elk Creek logging crew at rest. Elk Creek ran into Mud Creek flowing down from Mt. Shasta east of McCloud. Unlike the mill workers who lived in town, most loggers lived in the camps in the woods (see Page 36).

24. Much of the forest land around McCloud was relatively flat and provided a solid footing for horses. Log carts called "big wheels" were used to drag downed timber a short distance to railroad landings. Positioned between the wheels, the log was chained at one end to the raised cart tongue. The pull of the horses on the tongue levered the front of the log off the ground, enabling it to be dragged.

25. "Swampers" cleared rough roads in the woods for the big wheels. The large wheel diameter, up to eleven feet, was necessary to get the cart and the log across small ditches, debris, and rocks. Depending on conditions, two, four, six or more horses pulled the big wheels.

26. The Perry Log Cart was used extensively by McCloud. Similar designs were constructed in the railroad shops. Miller took many pictures of big wheels and they were popular subjects for post cards.

27. Steam tractors came into use in the logging camps by 1900 but horses continued to work until the mid-1920s when they were gradually replaced by motorized caterpillar tractors. Four-wheeled steam tractors designed for farm work were not as suitable for rough logging roads as this three-wheeler built by the Daniel Best Steam Traction Company, San Leandro, California.

28. The true workhorse of logging camps in Miller's era was the steam donkey. Developed in the late 1880s, it was essentially a wood-fired vertical steam engine driving a winch, The steam donkey derived from maritime steam engines of the same name used on wharves to load and off-load cargo from ships.

29. Steam donkeys were mounted on huge log sleds and moved as needed by winching themselves along the forest floor. Larger machines, called bull donkeys, were set up at a landing to control logs on a chute. Bull donkeys had larger drums for wire rope and usually horizontal capstans that kept the machine from twisting out of position as it pulled a heavy load.

30. Logs linked end to end by steel dogs formed a "train" pulled slowly along a chute by the bull donkey. The chute here crosses a ravine bridged by log cribbing. This and the next three shots Miller made in the summer of 1908 for the Northern California Lumber Company on Cottonwood Creek near Hilt.

31. Another view of the same log chute crossing a ravine. The chute, often called a pole road, can be seen as a series of smaller logs or poles laid end to end forming a continuous "v" groove. The last log on the train, called the pig, was flattened on top to carry supplies back up the chute. A man rode the pig down to the landing, ready to signal the donkey operator if he saw anything amiss. To signal, he tapped a metal rod on the low-voltage electric wire strung alongside the chute.
(See Page 123)

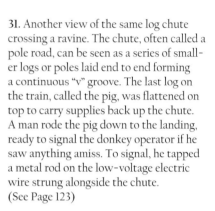

32. A big steam yarding donkey on Cottonwood Creek set up to control the stream of logs coming down the chute to the landing. The wire rope had to be pulled to the top of the chute after each log train by a team of horses. Alternately, the wire rope was hauled back by a lighter cable on a second winch drum which passed around a pulley at the upper end of the chute.

33. As the logs reached the landing, a second steam donkey pulled them off the chute and positioned them to continue their journey on another chute. By means of steam donkeys, upright king posts, and pulleys, heavy logs could be efficiently maneuvered by skilled operators

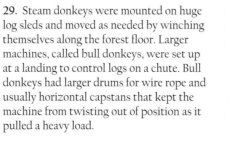

34. When the McCloud River Lumber Company extended a spur off the main line, they sent out a track-laying crew. The flatcars here are loaded with ties made at the mill and new rails sent over from Sisson, circa 1907. The steel rails often were pulled up and reused on new spurs as the camps were relocated.

38. Mealtime *al fresco* at a logging camp cafeteria line, McCloud River Lumber Company around 1907. Its not hard to spot the boss of this operation.

35. Portable camp buildings, shown here mounted on flatcars, followed the rails to the new campsite at a fresh stand of timber.

39. Mess tent off a camp kitchen of the McCloud River Lumber Company. Each camp was responsible for its own commissary and kitchen, and most had reputations as good feeders. Lumberjacks prodigious appetites were legendary and high-protein, well cooked meals were a requirement for high productivity.

36. The McCloud River Lumber Company maintained as many as five logging camps. This is No.1. The designations, 1, 2, and so on, followed where ever the camp happened to be located. Amenities included rustic family cabins, bachelor dormitories or tents, store houses, commissary, and cook house. Some camps remained on site for years, others were relocated within months.

40. Parbuckling logs onto flatcars with a bull donkey, Ash Creek Camp. Parbuckling was an old maritime trick for rolling heavy barrels up an incline. A wire rope from the donkey was fed over the flatcar and fastened to a log on the opposite side. When the rope was wound in, the log inched its way up the incline onto the flatcar. Each log was parbuckled and secured in succession until the car was loaded.

37. Here, loggers at Camp No. 1, McCloud River Lumber Company, pose for Miller around 1906. A camp crew consisted of specialized teams including fallers, buckers and trimmers, swampers, and teamsters.

41. Parbuckling from another view. The logs have been dragged to the landing by big wheels and yarded into position by a steam donkey. Miller shot this and previous view as part of documenting the production of lumber and of camp life.

42. Wherever anything remotely resembling a road could be made, a big steam tractor could carry massive log loads to the railroad landing. Here, a Best road engine pulls a four-wheeled wagon, sometimes called a bummer, barely visible behind the stump at left, ca.1910. A big advantage of steam tractors over horses was readily available wood for fuel, rather than animal feed that had to be purchased..

43. Another method of getting logs onto flatcars, speedier than parbuckling, was the McGiffert log loader. This McGiffert with a fixed boom lifts logs that have been dragged to the landing by big wheels. The McGiffert was essentially a bull donkey mounted on a steel frame that straddled the tracks. A set of wheels allowed the loader to move as needed along the tracks. When the McGiffert was ready to work, the wheels were raised and the machine came to rest on four frame posts that acted as stabilizing jacks.

44. No photographer can resist a trestle, Miller was no exception. Trestle shots were the pin ups of the logging camps and popular with tourists. Here, the 15 spot pulling a train of McCloud River Lumber Company logs pauses on the wooden trestle near Black Fox Mountain east of McCloud.

45. The low trestle east of Bartle of the McCloud River Railroad, engine No.14 up front pulling logs to the sawmill at McCloud.

46. Loading logs onto a flatcar, Lamoine Lumber and Trading Company, 1906. Here, the logs are rolled up onto the pile by means of a king post set up on the opposite side and a steam donkey just out of the picture. One end of each log has been "sniped" or trimmed to prevent it from snagging as it slides down a log chute.

47. One of many trestles of the Lamoine Lumber and Trading Company narrow-gauge railroad, 1906. The Company's entire complement of locomotives is in this log train picture, the 2-spot Shay up front, and "Maud," the 1-spot Climax, pushing at the rear.

48. Charles Miller was not an official Southern Pacific photographer, but that didn't prevent him from taking shots along the line. Here, he caught Shasta Springs' resort depot around 1902, showing from left to right, the bottling works, depot, and spring house. An incline railway leads from the rear of the spring house up to a resort hotel, natatorium or bath house, apartments, and a cluster of cottages.

49. Shasta Springs in winter. Miller returned to the same spot to show a Southern Pacific rotary snow plow pushed by a steam locomotive clearing tracks past the spring house. Southern Pacific passenger trains stopped at Shasta Springs to let travelers sample the water.

50. Big Canyon is a deep rift running down the southwest slope of Mt. Shasta. The Southern Pacific tracks, shown here with a passenger train around 1910, crossed Big Canyon between Cantara and Mott. This original wooden trestle later was replaced by landfill. Uphill from this, the McCloud River Railroad crossed Big Canyon by means of a huge culvert and landfill. See Page 70.

51. To cope with heavy snows, the McCloud River Railroad built its own wedge snow plow around 1905. Miller caught up with it at Sisson being pushed by two locomotives, No.11 and No.12.

52. Five McCloud River Railroad locomotives pushing the wedge bucker plow following a heavy storm, January 1914. When snow got too deep and heavy for the plow to push aside, the railroad had to turn to Southern Pacific for help.

53. Southern Pacific Railroad had a rotary snow plow capable of cutting through engine-deep snow. After clearing their main-line tracks, Southern Pacific would make the rotary available for a small rental fee to the McCloud line. Here, the rotary clears tracks at the McCloud depot.

54. Miller was commissioned in 1908 to document the Northern California Lumber Company operation near Hilt. The sawmill drew logs from the pond, which was kept supplied by a railroad that ran two miles up Cottonwood Creek, and by a log chute, shown at right.

55. The log dump for the mill on Cottonwood Creek. Charles Miller caught the action as an overhead cable, pulled by a steam donkey out of the picture, tripped a release on the flatcar that allowed logs to roll free into the pond.

56. The original Scott and Van Arsdale sawmill at McCloud is seen from the rear with Mt. Shasta as a backdrop. Rough cut green lumber emerges from the mill and is loaded onto flatcars for the trip to nearby drying yards.

57. This view of McCloud from atop the old sawmill shows smoke from the new mill in the distance. The railroad depot is out of the picture to the left. Lumber drying yards and storage are at right.

58. A millpond to serve the new mill at McCloud under construction in 1905-06. An earthen and log dam is raised around the site and filled with water diverted from Squaw Valley Creek. Railroad tracks, laid along one edge of the pond, serve as a log dump.

59. The completed new pond basking in the reflected glory of Mt. Shasta was photographed by Miller around 1907. Workers' bunkhouse No.3 is at right and a string of empty flatcars rests on the pond dam.

60. The new mill complex at the north side of McCloud, shown here around 1908, comprised the steam power house beneath the tall stack at left, the box factory behind it, the planning mill in center with a warehouse behind it, and a lumber shed at right.

61. The McCloud River Lumber Company built a sawmill and permanent camp on Ash Creek northeast of McCloud in 1899 as the Company expanded. The mill and a vast amount of lumber, shown here with Ash Creek Butte in the background, burned in 1903 and was not rebuilt. Logging, however, continued around Ash Creek for years.

62. Mill workers, including young boys, posed for Miller's camera at the second sawmill in McCloud.

63. McCloud school, built in 1904, is shown with students and teachers around 1908. This building was closed in 1928 when a new school superceded it.

64. Northern California Lumber Company officials pose with thirty-inch wide planks cut at their mill on Cottonwood Creek near Hilt in the summer of 1908. This yard had a little narrow gauge railroad with wooden rails to move lumber around. These premium-grade white pine planks, three inches thick, were often made into kitchen drain boards for new houses.

65. Inside the mill, a big pine log rests against the bandsaw in this setup for Miller's camera. The black board at left carries the sawyer's notes indicating dimensions and quantities of lumber to be cut.

66. Bucking crew posing with their work. After the fallers dropped the tree, and the trimmers cleared it of branches, teams of buckers, cut, or "bucked" the downed timber with two-man crosscut saws into movable lengths, most commonly just over twenty feet or just over sixteen feet.

70. McCloud River Railroad locomotive No 9 and a short consist pausing at Big Canyon fill, ca.1904, shortly after the fill had been reconstructed following a big washout.

67. Crew in Upton with McCloud River Railroad passenger coach No.1. This coach also carried the mail and Wells Fargo express packages to and from McCloud.

71. Miller made this magnificent portrait of the No.11 resting near the McCloud depot shortly after the railroad took delivery from Baldwin Locomotive Works in 1904. This locomotive was the first oil burner for the McCloud River Railroad.

68. Company houses at McCloud with Mt. Shasta in the background. Company houses in McCloud varied in size and elegance, and were assigned according to an employee's rank within the Company. These, facing a grassy mall called Lawndale, were for executives.

72. Log train of the Northern California Lumber Company on its way to the mill at Cottonwood Creek, pulled by one of three Climax locomotives owned by the company.

69. The McCloud River Railroad depot in the center of town, around 1908. The 12-spot locomotive pulling coach No.1 keeps up a head of steam awaiting the daily passenger run between McCloud and Upton. This original depot, built in 1897, was demolished in 1929 and replaced with a new structure, which lasted until it burned in 1990.

73. Car 100, the private car of McCloud River Lumber Company president Queal behind the combine passenger coach, around 1907. This wooden car was used for special excursions and by special guests including William Randolph Hearst and family.

74. Camp No.4, McCloud River Lumber Company in 1914. Locomotive No.7 pulling a dormitory car similar to the others on a siding. The residents are members of the Shaeffer, Haines, and Ackley families.

75. Locomotive No.12, originally the No.1, at the McCloud depot ready to depart on the daily passenger run to Upton around 1906.

76. McCloud depot with the Hotel Mc-Cloud in the background. Miller and most other visitors stayed at the big hotel with its 100 rooms, the only guest accommodations in town.

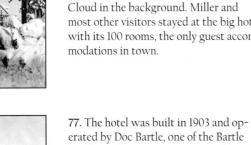

77. The hotel was built in 1903 and operated by Doc Bartle, one of the Bartle brothers who ran a stage stop and hotel east of McCloud known as Bartle's. The McCloud River Lumber Company took over this hotel around 1907. Destroyed by fire in 1915, the hotel was rebuilt with minor changes. Over the years it has undergone other modifications. After 1990 it became a bed and breakfast. Today it stands as a Nationally Registered Historic Landmark.

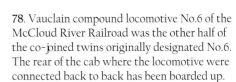

78. Vauclain compound locomotive No.6 of the McCloud River Railroad was the other half of the co-joined twins originally designated No.6. The rear of the cab where the locomotive were connected back to back has been boarded up.

79. A giant fir log, from Miller's 1908 album for the Northern California Lumber Company.

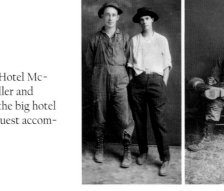

80. Two portraits by Miller, probably taken at his McCloud studio. The two men on the far left are identified as Charlie Linton and Frank Gibson.

81. Miller portraits in the woods. The two fallers pose with their essential equipment, double-bitted axes, crosscut saw, and whisky bottle filled with kerosene used to lubricate the saw. The water boy at left filled a vital job supplying loggers with drinking water in the woods.

82. Bartle station, just over 18 miles east of McCloud, established in 1905 as the eastern terminus of the McCloud River Railroad. The stage stop and settlement founded by brothers Abraham and Jerome Bartle on the pioneer wagon road to the McCloud River was known as Bartle's.

86. This remarkable quadruple switchback on the Lamoine Lumber and Trading Company railroad climbed to Sanford Pass at 4,500 feet elevation west of Lamoine. The railroad contained miles of torturous turns, steep grades, and switchbacks to reach high timber, ca.1912.

83. Depot at Bartle station was built in 1905 to replace an older structure nearby. Station Agent Pete Miller (no relation to Charles Miller) rests in the chair at left.

87. Camp No.2 near the top of Slate Mountain on the Lamoine Lumber and Trading Company railroad. The 2-spot Shay pauses with a train of log flats. From its appearance, this camp could be relocated with short notice, ca.1912.

84. Lamoine, spelled LaMoine in Miller's time, on the Southern Pacific main line. Lamoine was a mill town serving The Lamoine Lumber & Trading Company founded in 1898 by the Coggins brothers. After new management took over in 1906, they hired Miller to make a photographic album of their operation. The upper Sacramento River winds through town with Slate Creek emptying into the river from the west.

88. Lamoine Lumber and Trading Company inspection engine, a 1904 Oldsmobile. The McCloud River Railroad in 1906 got a similar engine, a fifty-horsepower model made by Thomas Flyer. Tracks, particularly hastily-laid spur lines on poorly prepared road beds subject to heavy use, had to be inspected constantly.

85. Lamoine Lumber and Trading Company new locomotives No.1 and No.2. The narrow gauge tracks did not extend to the SP line at Lamoine but delivered logs to the head of a two-mile long flume which sent the logs down to a box factory and railroad siding at Lamoine.

89. These two 1880s vintage Southern Pacific locomotives from Southern Pacific hauling a wood train on the McCloud River Railroad game to grief on the Ash Creek line in 1900. Judging from the large tree atop the engine on the right, the runaway must have been spectacular.

90. Locomotive No. 6 derailed on the McCloud River Railroad, ca.1902. This experimental engine design by Baldwin Locomotive Works comprised two engines attached back to back to provide greater pulling power and flexibility. After demonstrating a tendency to jump the tracks, the engines were separated and assigned No. 5 and No.6. The unusual cage at center is a wood rack, positioned on the left side of both engine halves.

91. Results of a runaway north of Bartle. An early caption for this photo described it as a seventeen flatcar pileup.

92. Southern Pacific flatcars fitted with wood racks after a runaway on McCloud River Railroad tracks. The McCloud River Lumber Company did a steady business with Southern Pacific supplying cord wood for locomotives and ties.

93. Locomotive No.5 in trouble again, McCloud River Railroad (see 78 and 90). Despite dramatic runaways and exasperating derailments, no McCloud engine was ever damaged beyond repair. This engine's twin, No.6, survived until after World War II working in the Kaiser shipyards at Richmond, California.

94. Shortly after 1900 the automobile made its presence felt in the Mt. Shasta area. A gated toll road was graded through the woods from Castle Crags east toward McCloud. The road followed the old Red Cross Lumber Company railroad bed (the rails had been pulled up and reused by the McCloud River Railroad) along Soda Creek to the McCloud River. Wealthy sportsmen drove their automobiles from the SP station at Castle Crags to their private fishing resorts.

95. The toll road in 1908, with executives of the Northern California Lumber Company, which leased and logged the Soda Creek Tract. Through his work for Scott and Van Arsdale of the McCloud River Lumber Company, Miller became acquainted with men such as William Randolph Hearst and Clarence Waterhouse, and was invited to photograph their McCloud River estates.

96. The McCloud River with the Clarence Waterhouse residence in the distance.

97. The Burns and Waterhouse residence on the McCloud River. Clarence Waterhouse, a prominent California businessman maintained this fishing lodge and compound near the residence of Charles Stetson Wheeler, attorney for William Randolph Hearst.

98. Hearst was so taken by the McCloud River region, he acquired over 50,000 acres and built a fishing lodge for his mother Phoebe Apperson Heart, a trout fishing enthusiast. He hired architect Bernard Maybeck to build the castle Hearst called Wyntoon. Miller photographed it under construction in 1903.

99. Wyntoon completed, ca.1905. It burned in 1930 and Hearst hired architect Julia Morgan to build a new version for Hearst and his mistress Marion Davies. Davies reputedly referred to it as "Spitoon." Hearst also retained Julia Morgan to design his castle on the California coast at San Simeon.

100. Aside from commissions from the logging companies, Miller kept busy photographing scenic views for his postcard business. This is Big Springs, an underground tributary that flows into the McCloud River down from Mt. Shasta through a basaltic aquafer. Miller found the river not only photogenic but conveniently close to good fishing.

101. Black Butte, a volcanic relic from an ancient eruption, in wonderful contrast to its neighbor, Mt. Shasta. After Charles Miller moved his studio to Klamath Falls, Oregon in 1909, he returned often to photograph the Mt. Shasta region.

The McCloud River Lumber Company
McCLOUD, CAL.

MANUFACTURERS OF
WHITE AND SUGAR PINE LUMBER
LATH - MOULDINGS
BEVELLED SIDING
SASH AND DOOR CUTTINGS
BOX SHOOKS.

ANNUAL CAPACITY

SAW MILLS	100,000,000 Ft.
LATH MILLS	16,000,000 Pcs.
PLANING MILLS	75,000,000 Ft.
DRY KILNS	35,000,000 Ft.
BOX FACTORY	20,000,000 Ft.
CUTTING FACTORY	15,000,000 Ft.
MOULDINGS	155 Car Loads

| SHED CAPACITY | 15,000,000 Ft. |
| YARD CAPACITY | 65,000,000 Ft. |

OUR ENTIRE PLANT - SAW MILLS, PLANING MILLS, FAC-
TORIES, DRY KILNS, LUMBER SHEDS, ETC., COVERS
OVER 700 ACRES.
OUR LUMBER YARDS ALONE COVER OVER 50 ACRES.

OFFICES   MILLS   FACTORIES
McCLOUD, CAL.

WE SOLICIT YOUR INQUIRES.

Post Card

BLACK AND WHITE

McCloud River R. R.

1108

McCLOUD RIVER RAILROAD COMPANY.
CONDUCTOR'S RECEIPT CHECK.
D. M. SWOBE,
Traffic Manager.

AUDITOR'S STUB
McCLOUD RIVER RAILROAD COMPANY

FORM
8253

McCloud from atop the sawmill, Charles Miller, 1909.

CHARLES MILLER AND McCLOUD

The company town of McCloud was new when Charles Miller first set up his photographic studio there in 1905. Most of the structures including the sawmill had been built within the previous eight years. The town served one purpose: the needs of the McCloud River Lumber Company. In exchange, the Company provided all that the town and its residents needed. McCloud was a product of the Company, by the Company, and for the Company. The McCloud River Lumber Company built and owned every store, every house, every road and facility. Residents, almost exclusively workers and their families, called it Mother McCloud. Although nothing survives of his business records or personal correspondence, Charles Miller and Mother McCloud evidently got on well.

The Company managers, rightfully proud of their enterprise, promoted and advertised McCloud to the outside world. Scott and Van Arsdale commissioned local photographers including Charles Miller and Jervie Eastman of Sisson and the Hicks-Chatten Engraving Company to shoot publicity photos for their operation. Miller produced photo postcards and souvenirs to be offered to the public. After Miller moved to McCloud he became known as the "McCloud photographer." While it is unclear if Miller actually ever became a Company employee, he was provided a studio and darkroom in town, designed to his specifications. For this he paid a modest rent of $50 per year. Since he produced photos at the same time for competing logging companies, probably he worked on commission for McCloud.

The McCloud River Lumber Company prospered in those years, building in 1899 a new sawmill on Ash Creek at the base of Mt. Shasta. Three years later the mills were turning out 400,000 board feet of lumber every twenty-four hours and maintained a payroll of between 600 and 800 men. By 1902 work was under way for a second larger mill in McCloud, greatly increasing the Company's output of finished lumber and lumber products. The new mill, the Company boasted, would be one of the most modern and thoroughly equipped bandsaw mills in the country. Miller kept busy for the Company recording the expansion, the town, and its people. He took his camera to the logging camps and photographed the men at work, fallers, trimmers, swampers, teamsters and steam donkey operators. He made portraits of

115

This little mill was owned by McKea, Vance, and Pierson, a partnership set up in 1895 at Pebble in Squaw Valley. John McKea took over his partners' interests in 1898 and went on to form the Esperanza Lumber and Timber Company, a leading lumber producer. By 1902 McKea owned two mills in the upper McCloud River region as well as a summer resort on the river known as Fowler's. Unidentified photographer.

everyone from foreman to water boy. In McCloud, he made a detailed photographic record of sawmill operations, everyday activities, special events and construction projects.

Even though the sawmill town of McCloud was new, logging in the area was not. Small sawmills around Mt. Shasta dated back to the late 1850s, perhaps earlier. Evidence indicates that the McCloud River and the wooded country nearby got its name from Alexander McLeod, a trapper for the Hudson's Bay Company, who first explored the region in 1827. Another version, however, claims its namesake was Ross McCloud, an early pioneer and settler. Either way, the little town that bears the McCloud name today began as Vandale, a name derived from that of its builder William Wilson Van Arsdale. He and his partner George W. Scott would have called the town McCloud but that name was taken. The Southern Pacific Railroad had a little station south of Sisson in Strawberry Valley called McCloud.

Scott and Van Arsdale, both engineers and entrepreneurs, had come to Strawberry Valley shortly after completion of the railroad link through there in 1887. Strawberry Valley, a large plateau near the headwaters of the Sacramento River, was home to early settlers including Justin Sisson, who ran a trading post and stage coach stop. The railroad, upon reaching the valley, laid out a town site and station and named it Sisson in his honor. The town of Sisson (renamed Mt. Shasta in 1922) became the jumping off point to reach the McCloud River basin to the south and east of Mt. Shasta. Both Scott and Van Arsdale probably first experienced the McCloud River country as guests of fellow Bohemian Club members from San Francisco. The river was noted for its excellent trout fishing, and the forested valleys for their serene splendor. William Randolph Hearst and other San Francisco notables had private resorts secluded along the river, and owned large nearby tracts of land. It was a rich man's paradise, where one could do as one pleased in the company of like-minded people and where one's conduct went unreported.

Strawberry Valley also became the center for early logging operations. The slopes were heavily wooded and close to the railroad. Small sawmills sprang up and began shipping lumber to San Francisco on the new railroad. One of these at Upton, a settlement two miles north of Sisson, was owned and operated by the Siskiyou Mercantile and Lumber Company, the largest business in the area other than the Southern Pacific Railroad. George Scott and William Van Arsdale took over management of the Upton company, its sawmill, and the store in Sisson. With an infusion of capital and enthusiasm by the new partners and managers, Siskiyou Mercantile was prime for expansion.

Sisson in Strawberry Valley around 1907. Miller photo.

Freight wagons on the Davis Road en route from Glass Mountain to Pumice Stone, July 3, 1909. This road stretched from Laird's Landing on Lower Klamath Lake to Bartle. Freight had to traverse the lake by boat, then by wagon to Bartle, then by rail to Sisson and the main line of the Southern Pacific Railroad.

By the early 1890s, locally available trees had been cut and marketed, and other logging companies had bought up nearby timber rights. Scott and Van Arsdale had to reach further to keep their enterprise going. Their mill at Upton, hampered by inadequate water supply, had a limited future. The partners turned east, where vast tracts of timberland nourished by the McCloud River carpeted miles of relatively flat terrain about 3,500 feet elevation at the base of Mt. Shasta. Scott and Van Arsdale were not the first to recognize the logging potential of the McCloud River basin. Several small sawmills had tried it with varying degrees of success. The Southern Pacific Railroad had eyed the timberlands and surveyed a railroad from Dunsmuir to the McCloud River country. The Red Cross Lumber Company, working on Soda Creek near Dunsmuir actually started construction of a railroad along Soda Creek to the McCloud River, but completed only four miles of it.

A man with the unlikely name of Ambrose Friday George, former superintendent of Southern Pacific's Shasta Division, had entered the lumber business in 1891 when he reopened a defunct mill near Dusmuir. The next year he relocated this mill to Squaw Valley Creek, a tributary of the McCloud River ten miles east of Strawberry Valley. Friday George envisioned a railroad between the two points but that would taken capital well beyond his reach. To get his McCloud River lumber to the Southern Pacific main line at Mott, Friday George had to haul it over ten miles. He cleared and graded a rudimentary wagon road for ox teams but it traversed a rise of over a thousand feet before dropping down to Mott at the upper end of the Sacramento River canyon. When the animals proved unprofitable, he tried a huge steam-powered road tractor, shipped up from San Francisco. While it could haul heavier loads, the steam tractor was no match for wet or freezing weather. High operating and maintenance costs on his road, plus a depression in the lumber industry that beset California in 1894, drove Friday George and his mill to bankruptcy.

In 1895 Scott and Van Arsdale picked up Friday George's operation at auction. The new owners determined to fulfill the long-anticipated venture, a railroad from the Southern Pacific main line to the McCloud River country. They planned a modern sawmill

Top left: Logging near the McCloud River with ox teams, ca.1895. Unidentified photographer.

Left: Loading pine logs on wagons around 1895. Unidentified photographer.

on the site of Friday George's old mill, reinvigorated the little village around the mill on Squaw Valley Creek, and named it Vandale. The following spring, flush with money from new investors, Scott and Van Arsdale began surveying the route their new rails would take. They already owned a mill and box factory at Upton, and found that from there to Vandale would require only twelve miles of track including two switchbacks to avoid building trestles over deep ravines. By summer, work had begun from their sawmill at Upton heading east across the lower slopes of the mountain. Trees were felled along the way to feed the Upton mill, providing a revenue source as work progressed. At the same time, teams of horses transported equipment from Upton for the new sawmill at Vandale so when the rails finally reached the new mill, it would be ready for service.

Winter snows shut down construction for 1896, allowing the stockholders to formalize their new enterprise. Incorporated respectively as the McCloud River Lumber Company and the McCloud River Railroad Company, the San Francisco directors envisioned a bright future. They controlled among other assets 185,000 acres of standing timber, mostly sugar pine, yellow pine, and red fir. The parent corporation remained Scott and Van Arsdale, with huge lumber yards in San Francisco, Stockton and San Jose. The new plant, McCloud River Lumber Company, fit in the family tree as but one of the Company's facilities. Others included the mill at Upton and the Siskiyou Lumber and Mercantile Company store at Sisson.

That winter the tracks extended only four of the dozen miles from Upton, but the last leg into Vandale would be constructed beginning the following spring. A mogul locomotive, purchased from the California Railway, was renamed Number 1, and stood ready to pull the first load of McCloud lumber. Delays and complications, however, kept the line from reaching Vandale on schedule. At last, on July 21, 1897, the job was done. Within a month, lumber from the mill began rolling toward Upton to link up with the Southern Pacific main line. Passengers and freight began moving east from Sisson to Vandale, to continue on by horse-drawn stage and wagon. Southern Pacific cooperated by selling tickets on the new line and by changing the name of their McCloud station to Azalea. Thus the McCloud name was snapped up by Scott and Van Arsdale. Vandale became McCloud.

Bottom right: Lacking a railroad, Friday George transported his lumber to market with a steam tractor similar to this 1896 model. Unidentified photographer.

This unidentified sawmill could be the Friday George works on Squaw Valley Creek.

LIFE IN McCLOUD

The town expanded under total Company control. Streets were laid out and houses built as needed. A commercial center, complete with hotel, company store, offices, churches, a school, hospital and pool hall, clustered around the depot on Main Street. The buildings were architecturally straightforward box designs in neat rows, with forty-five-degree gable roofs to deflect deep snows, and built, naturally, with local lumber. No brick or stone. All doors and window sashes were made in the sash mill. Workers were charged modest rent. Their houses could be relocated within the town complex at the discretion of the Company.

McCloud was a model town, a fine example of careful planning and genuine concern by management for its workers. It was one of the first small towns in California to provide electricity to every home. The Company built a modern sewerage system and provided water free of charge and cord wood for heating at a nominal charge. In an ironic twist, McCloud's modernity played a part in a near disaster. In the summer of 1903, typhoid fever broke out in McCloud and quickly spread throughout the community, striking down loggers, mill workers and their families, railroad employees and executives. Among those who died from the epidemic was the son of the general manager of the McCloud River Railroad. The cause of the outbreak eventually was traced to contaminated milk delivered to McCloud by an unscrupulous dairyman. He had diluted his milk with water from a source contaminated by the town's sewerage system. Over time the spread of typhoid was checked. Charles Miller, despite his frequent visits to McCloud, had escaped the fever, so he thought. The typhoid incident kept tourists, fearful of another outbreak, away from McCloud for months afterward. Unfortunately for Miller, it did not deter him from visiting the town. In the fall of 1904, the *Sisson Headlight* reported that the photographer C.R. Miller had been suffering for two weeks with typhoid fever, but that he was recovering. Miller was able to return to work temporarily, but his weakened condition sent him back to Portland to rest and regain his strength.

Top left: Typical Company houses, Quincey Street, McCloud. Yeager photo, 1922.

Left: The McCloud hospital, built in 1907 with 25 beds, operating room, maternity ward, and pharmacy. McCloud's first physician, Dr. Legge, later taught industrial medicine at the University of California. Photo by Miller, ca.1908.

Life in McCloud was simple in the days when Charles Miller first arrived. Men worked at the sawmill in shifts, or in the box and sash factory. Some worked for the railroad. The men lived in the bachelors' dormitory or, if they were married, in the little box houses. Their wives tended the homes and raised the kids. Citizens of McCloud attended churches, any of several denominations, went to the community dance hall, celebrated holidays and held picnics and excursions into the woods. Some went fishing on the nearby McCloud River, famous then as now for the excellent quality and abundance of trout.

Men in the logging camps usually lived there in tents and small cabins. They tended to be a more transient group, moving from camp to camp wherever work could be found. Although the loggers had varied skills and performed specific operations, their job collectively was to provide a steady flow of saw logs to the mill. Each camp had a foreman whose saw to it that the goal was met. The Company railroad would build a spur line to the timber stand, the camp was erected and logging commenced. The close-in trees were felled first, then cut or "bucked" into manageable lengths, then dragged or carried to the railroad landing. As the loggers moved farther into the woods beyond the reach of horse and wagon, either the rails had to be extended or log chutes had to be constructed to get the cut logs to the rails. Eventually after a period of weeks or months, the camp was moved. Rails were pulled up and the spur abandoned. A new spur pushed to a fresh timber stand. The camp structures were loaded on flat cars and delivered to the new site. Over the years the Company built and recycled hundred of miles of rail spurs.

Life and work in McCloud might seem comfortable when viewed from our vantage point a century in the future. But it was fraught with hazards and hardships. There were no child labor laws. Boys as young as nine or ten worked in the mills, doing routine and sometimes dangerous repetitious work. The hospital in McCloud seems large for a town of only seven or eight hundred residents. But the beds were frequently filled with men who had suffered horrendous injuries. Aside from railroad accidents (two trainmen were killed even before the tracks reached McCloud), logging in the woods presented many opportunities to lose an arm or leg, an eye, or worse. Log chains and wire ropes could snap without warning, lashing out with lightning ferocity. Trees could and did fall the wrong way. Men worked unprotected from snapping branches, rattlesnakes, disease,

Right: The McCloud home of General Manager Queal of the McCloud River Railroad. ca.1906. Miller photo.

The McCloud River Lumber Company store and pay office, ca.1905. Miller Photo.

and harsh weather. In the mills were other perils. Pond workers risked their lives daily balanced atop floating logs as they pushed them to the mill chute. As the logs were drawn up the chute and pulled through the rapidly moving band saw, any rocks imbedded in the bark that failed to dislodge could shatter a band saw blade, sending deadly steel shrapnel flying inside the mill house. Handling wet, heavy lumber was daily routine, where slight miscalculation could crush a hand or foot, or drive a spike-sized splinter through flesh.

Dangerous working conditions were not unique to McCloud or any particular industry, but were intrinsic to early nineteenth century life. Considering the standards of the time, Mother McCloud did a good job of caring for her people. Families stayed, men worked with pride, babies were born and grew up in McCloud. Work proceeded harmoniously for the most part. Racial and ethnic prejudice played a role in early McCloud, as in every other town and city in America. Chinese were not welcome. Due to a labor shortage, Chinese workers were employed building the railroad but, at the insistence of non-Chinese workers, were not hired in the mills or logging camps. Hispanic (and later, black) workers, small in number, lived in small enclaves of Company houses. Italian immigrants comprised an increasing percentage of mill workers. They lived in villages at the edge of McCloud on Company land but usually in ramshackle home-made cabins. Miller's photographs show workers of all nationalities side by side, and school children seemingly unaffected by their diverse backgrounds. Visitors even toured the Italian villages just to see the arts and crafts native to the old country. But just as the town of McCloud lies in the shadow of a dormant volcano, it contained within it dormant ethnic discontent that would erupt one day.

Left: Poling logs to the sawmill chute in the McCloud millpond, from a stereo, attributed to Miller, ca.1902.

122

Left: Chuting logs down to the mill on Slate Creek, Lamoine Lumber & Trading Company. This photo clearly illustrates some of the hazards faced by loggers in the woods. Miller photo, 1906.

Bottom: A good view by Miller, ca.1908, inside a McCloud sawmill and the machinery that transformed logs into cut lumber. The big steam engines that turned the band saw also powered the moving carriage and the generator that provided electricity to the mill. A separate steam powerhouse produced electric power for the town's residents free of charge.

In the summer of 1909, a crisis gripped McCloud, brought about by the inequity in pay between the Italians and non-Italian workers. Workers were not part of a trade union and, as salaries increased for some, Italian workers's pay stagnated. By 1909, almost two-thirds of McCloud mill workers were Italian and the pay discrepancy had become a sore point they wanted resolved.

Lack of action by the Company became intolerable and the Italians demanded an increase of twenty-five cents per day over their prevailing wage of $1.75 per day. President Queal was in Chicago at the time but representatives of the Company flatly refused the demand. The Italian leaders called a strike and threatened to stop all trains except those carrying the U.S. Mail. Threats and counter threats quickly escalated, and the Siskiyou County sheriff arrived with sixty deputies. Sensing eminent violence, newspapers around the state sent reporters to McCloud. Charles Miller, camera in hand, arrived from Klamath Falls to record events as they unfolded. Rumors had it that the Italians had seized the dynamite shed and had threatened to kill anyone trying to break the strike.

The sheriff requested assistance from the California National Guard. A special train was dispatched to McCloud from Sacramento with three infantry companies, a cavalry company, and a hospital corps detachment. The militia train, pushing flatcars manned by sharpshooters, rolled cautiously into McCloud on June third. Guardsmen, whose purpose was to keep the lid on an explosive situation, almost did the opposite when one of their number bayoneted an argumentative striker in the thigh. The reporters telegraphed their stories to the *Sacramento Union*, the *San Francisco Call*, and other newspapers describing in lurid detail how "the Latins now lust for blood." The Italian Consul in San Francisco called on the National Guard to protect the innocent Italians from violence. Residents of McCloud demanded protection from the Italian "mob." Adding to the tension, a noted San Francisco strike breaker, J. F. Farley, arrived on the scene. The standoff continued.

President Queal, who had arrived with the militia train, stood fast and declared the striking workers would be driven from town if they would not work. After several days of tense inaction by both sides, five of the strike leaders were arrested by the sheriff and taken to Sisson. That seemed to deflate the strike and further violence was averted. When the National Guard left town on the tenth of June, some disgruntled Italian workers did too, and shortly thereafter, Italian workers were granted a pay raise. The event became a footnote in McCloud history, the workers later all became unionized, and the Italian village remained for many years. Charles Miller's photographs became a popular series of postcards.

Top left: Italian workers organize in their "village."

Middle left: Italian workers march on Company headquarters.

Bottom Left: Sharpshooters on flatcars arrive in McCloud with the militia.

Top right: Officers and men of the Hospital Corps at McCloud.

Middle right: The Siskiyou County Sheriff handcuffs two of the strike leaders.

Below: The National Guard encampment near the McCloud lumber storage sheds.

All strike photos courtesy Heritage Junction Museum.

CHARLES MILLER AND THE RAILROAD

Charles Miller, like most western photographers, never met a railroad locomotive he didn't like. Commercial photographers liked to take pictures of engines and trains, in part, because the public liked to buy them. Trains symbolized progress, they provided muscle to industry and the primary means to get from one place to another. Steam locomotives were integral to American life. In 1900 almost every town in the country had rails passing through it and the mournful cry of the steam whistle was commonplace and welcome. Railroads usually were well run and well maintained, a source of pride for railroad workers and crews. The McCloud River Railroad was no exception. No passenger was ever injured or killed on a McCloud train, although crewmen and track workers were not so fortunate.

By 1902 the railroad had thirty miles of standard gauge track, another thirty miles in logging spurs, eight locomotives and two hundred cars, mainly flatcars. When Miller left McCloud in 1909, the railroad had fourteen hard-working steam locomotives in service and had added many more miles of spur tracks reaching deep into the woods. There was little glamour to the outfit, no high-speed express trains, posh Pullman cars or fancy diners. It existed to get logs to the mills and McCloud lumber to market. Passengers and freight were a necessary sideline. Its main line tracks in Miller's time, reached from Upton to McCloud, east to Bartle and beyond.

Miller had no difficulty persuading crews to stop long enough to have their picture taken with their engines. More formal portraits of trains and crews were staged by Miller for advertising purposes but Miller also made many photos of routine operations, the shops and roundhouse, and occasional train derailments.

HERITAGE JUNCTION MUSEUM

HERITAGE JUNCTION MUSEUM

Top left: McCloud No.4 was a Baldwin purchased new by the McCloud River Railroad in 1898. Here she is decked out for an excursion around 1905. Miller photo.

Bottom left: McCloud No.5 after being separated from its co-joined twin. The other half (Page 78) kept the No. 6 designation. These wood burners each carried their fuel stacked in a side rack, hidden from view in this Miller photo, ca.1905.

Miller made this photo around 1909 of a Southern Pacific locomotive pulling a train of logs north of Weed.

This trestle about two miles east of Bartle on the McCloud River Railroad was popular with photographers. Not as dramatic as some trestles on the Southern Pacific Shasta Route, it nevertheless presented a graceful curve and wooded backdrop. Here the No.8, newly converted to oil burning, pulls a big load of pine logs to the mill at McCloud. This locomotive survives today as a static display at the Sierra Nevada town of Ione after many years of logging service. Miller photo.

The No.9 and her crew pose for Miller around 1905. This photo illustrates a typical consist for the McCloud River Railroad. Two locomotives, one at each end, provided sufficient power to haul a big load of lumber over steep grades, and solved the problem of the Signal Butte switchback between McCloud and Upton. Trains went forward out of McCloud to the switchback, then reversed directions for the remainder of the twelve-mile trip. With an engine facing forward at both ends, the train never had to run backward. Here, the engine at the other end is probably No.8, sister of No.9, both shown in their wood burning days.

McCloud No.8 on the Big Canyon fill between McCloud and Upton some- time after 1901. Seeking to avoid building a trestle across the steep ravine, the Company made a switchback above it. Later, the gap was bridged by installing a culvert and filling the gap. Chinese laborers built a succession of water flumes from springs high above the canyon. Water was collected in holding basins and forced under high-pressure to dislodge rocks and earth, a process similar to hydraulic mining. The debris collected behind a dam and was compacted into the roadbed. Later floods washed out the fill but it was rebuilt around 1902. Miller photo.

Baldwin-built No.10 was originally a wood burner when McCloud acquired her new in 1901. The big diamond stack arrester was removed when the locomotive was converted to oil, as shown here. Wood fuel for a logging locomotive seemed an obvious choice but providing an adequate supply was time consuming. Hand feeding wood into the firebox was more difficult than pumping oil into the burners. Burning wood also necessitated bulky spark arresters on the smoke stack to reduce the risk of forest fires. The McCloud line completed the transition from wood, or lump oil as it was jokingly called, to oil in 1921. The little hinged damper at the top of the stack in this photo was installed to keep rain and snow out and trap heat in the boiler when the engine rested overnight. The headlight mounted at the rear of the tender helped when the engine ran backward due to the Signal Butte switchback. Miller photo.

Miller photographed the new No.15 for the McCloud River Railroad in 1907. The caboose is named "Shasta."

McCloud No.18, built by Baldwin in 1914, was an oil burner. Before the new engine was delivered to McCloud, she was put on display at the 1915 Pamama-Pacific International Exposition in San Francisco. Here at the McCloud depot, the No.18 still looks brand new. No.18 was sold in 1956 to the Yreka Western Railroad, repurchased in the late 1990s, and returned to operating condition by the McCloud Company. No.18 along with steam locomotive No.25 is stored at the McCloud Railway Shop. Miller photo.

No. 15 a few years after the photo opposite, when the McCloud name had been abbreviated with initial letters. The crew, obviously proud of their well-kept engine, are posed at the McCloud depot with Bartle Station Agent Pete Miller (third from left), and are identified by Charles Miller as "Spencer, Demers, Miller, Dennis, Nord, and Roe."

THE BIG STORM

Winter snows are part of life at Mt. Shasta. For logging and railroading, deep snow presents obvious problems. Trains cannot run through it and loggers can't cut trees in it. The business of lumbering, however, depends on a steady supply of logs and a steady flow of products to market. The logging camps would stay in operation as long as possible, then shut down for the winter. The mill would cut lumber until it ran out of logs. But the railroad carried freight and passengers as well as logs and lumber. Early on, Scott and Van Arsdale had determined to make McCloud River Railroad a year round, money-making operation.

In light snows, a small blade called a pilot plow was attached to the front of the locomotives. Occasionally, however, the snowfall in a winter season might reach fifteen or twenty feet, enough to halt everything. The railroad at first couldn't afford its own snow removal equipment beyond the pilot plows, so it relied on manpower (with shovels) and rented snow plows from the Southern Pacific Railroad. Southern Pacific, with its equipment stored at Dunsmuir only twenty miles from McCloud, was happy to oblige whenever it didn't need the plows to clear its own main line tracks. By 1902 the McCloud River Railroad had its own snow plows including a big wooden wedge or "bucker" plow. The bucker could slice through deep snow and push it aside to allow passage of the trains. But it had its limits and, when those limits were exceeded, the bucker tended to derail itself. In exceptionally heavy snowfalls, the only machine capable of clearing the tracks was the big rotary plows of the Southern Pacific. Again, Southern Pacific came to the rescue, clearing tracks for a fee from Sisson to McCloud and beyond as needed.

Photographers, Miller included, found snow removal fascinating. The contrast of dark machines struggling through white blankets of snow made for dramatic shots. Most spectacular of all was the rotary, a whirring monster pushed by straining steam locomotives, boring through mountains of snow and flinging it aside in a wide, highly photogenic arc. Miller happened to be down from Klamath Falls in Sisson in late December 1912, when a massive storm blew down from the Siskiyous. Snow began to fall in prodigious quantity. For days it snowed. The big bucker plow of the McCloud River Railroad was brought out in an attempt to

Top left: Engine crews in 1898 wave from atop their locomotives behind the Southern Pacific bucker plow. Unidentified photographer.

Bottom left: Workers attempt to clear ice that can cause the bucker plow to derail. Miller photo.

ROTARY SNOW PLOW ON McCLOUD RIVER R.R. CALIF.
302   © MILLER PHOTO Co

open the tracks to Sisson. For a few days, it did the job. Still more snow fell. By early January, the bucker could no longer cope. It slid off the tracks in the twelve-foot drifts at the summit. Word went out in Sisson that Southern Pacific would attempt to clear a path with their rotary. Charles Miller persuaded the railroad to let him go along. Another Sisson photographer, E. J. Lawless, followed on skis to capture the action. By the time the rotary reached McCloud, the town had been isolated for a week. Within two days of his return to Sisson, Miller had photo postcards of the rescue on sale.

In the winter of 1913-14 Miller was once again in McCloud when a winter storm set in, and he made dramatic photos of five locomotives attempting to remove snow (Pages 52-53). The photo postcards made from this event remained popular for years.

Top: The derailed bucker plow is rescued by the Southern Pacific rotary. Miller photo.

Top right: Miller braves the cold riding one of the locomotives pushing the rotary from Sisson toward McCloud, January 1914.

Right: An open path to McCloud. Miller photo.

Part of Charles Miller's work for the McCloud River Lumber Company was to document each step in the process of producing finished lumber products. To that end, he produced hundreds of detailed photographs, many of which became company promotional postcards. Here, fallers undercut a white pine to direct its fall. Above, a bucker demonstrates the technique of reducing the tree to manageable logs.

On the page opposite are samples of Miller's promotional postcards., ca.1906

No. 17—"Swamping" Roads for the "Big Wheels."

No. 18—"Rolling" or Separating Logs After Being "Bucked" or Cut Into Lengths.

No. 14—A White Pine Tree—"Felled," "Bucked," "Rolled" and "Swamped."

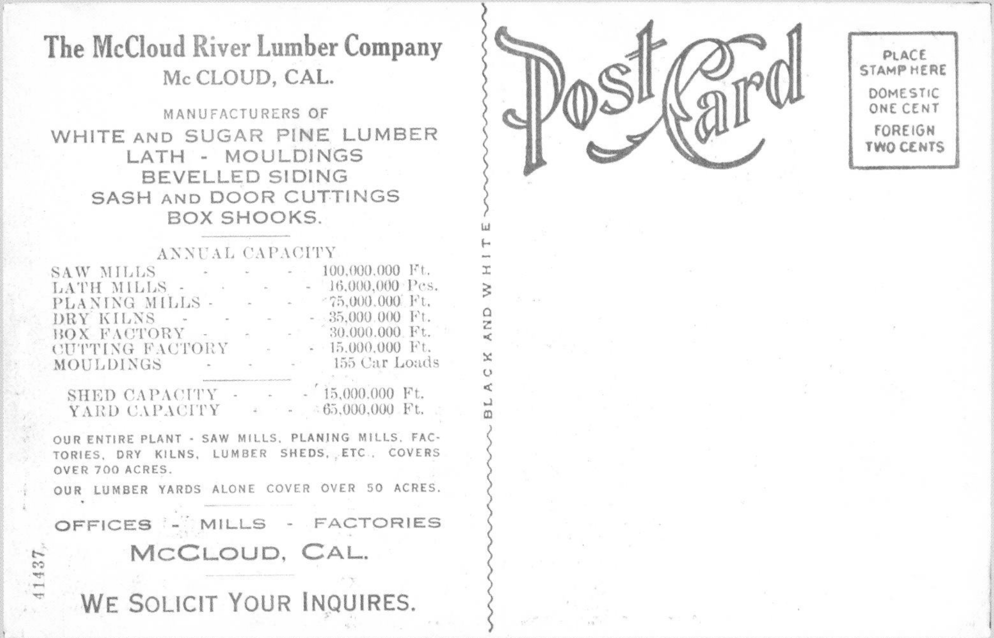

HERITAGE JUNCTION MUSEUM

The McCloud River Lumber Company
Mc CLOUD, CAL.

MANUFACTURERS OF
WHITE and SUGAR PINE LUMBER
LATH - MOULDINGS
BEVELLED SIDING
SASH and DOOR CUTTINGS
BOX SHOOKS.

ANNUAL CAPACITY

SAW MILLS	100,000,000 Ft.
LATH MILLS	16,000,000 Pcs.
PLANING MILLS	75,000,000 Ft.
DRY KILNS	35,000,000 Ft.
BOX FACTORY	30,000,000 Ft.
CUTTING FACTORY	15,000,000 Ft.
MOULDINGS	155 Car Loads

SHED CAPACITY	15,000,000 Ft.
YARD CAPACITY	65,000,000 Ft.

OUR ENTIRE PLANT - SAW MILLS, PLANING MILLS, FAC-
TORIES, DRY KILNS, LUMBER SHEDS, ETC. COVERS
OVER 700 ACRES.

OUR LUMBER YARDS ALONE COVER OVER 50 ACRES.

OFFICES - MILLS - FACTORIES
MCCLOUD, CAL.

WE SOLICIT YOUR INQUIRES.

41437

BLACK AND WHITE

Post Card

PLACE
STAMP HERE
DOMESTIC
ONE CENT
FOREIGN
TWO CENTS

The essential task of the loggers was to get trees out of the woods to the sawmill. Until the 1880s, the process was slow, dangerous, and labor intensive, with beasts of burden suffering under the yoke. The steam donkey with its wire rope and powerful winch relieved much of the need for animals. The logging railroad completed the modernization, allowing the loggers to extend their operations farther from the sawmill. Miller made these photographs around 1907 demonstrating the modern practices of the McCloud River Lumber Company.

As the log is dragged from the storage pond into the sawmill, water under high pressure displaced rocks and debris from the bark, reducing the danger of a shattered bandsaw blade. Imbedded steel wedges were a particular danger.

Right: A crew of Mill No.1, McCloud River Lumber Company, pose on the bull chain during a change of shift, ca.1908.

In the summer of 1906 Miller secured a major commission from the Lamoine Lumber and Trading Company, a rival of the McCloud Lumber Company. The Lamoine operation was on Slate Creek, which fed into the Sacramento River near the Southern Pacific stop at Lamoine. Logging the dense timber on steep terrain west of the Sacramento had proved to much for the original company and, in 1904, the operation was taken over by the Rosenberg Brothers out of Fresno. The reorganized operation built a narrow-gauge railroad to traverse the rugged mountains rising from Slate Creek. The line eventually comprised over seventy miles of switchback track and trestles but did not connect directly to the Southern Pacific main line. The first locomotive, a Climax, affectionately called "Maud," pulled a string of thirty wooden logging flat cars. In 1906, the Company added their second locomotive, a Shay, larger than Maud, but able to make the tight turns and steep grades of the railway. One of Miller's first photographs for the Lamoine Lumber and Trading Company is of the two little locomotives, clean and polished, and their crews equally spruced up for the occasion (Page 85). Miller produced an album with forty-five detailed photographs of the railroad, logging operations, and a few scenic views of Mt. Shasta.

The town of Lamoine suffered a fire in 1917 that also burned the mill. The lumber company, however, continued operations until 1922 when the lack of timber brought it to a halt.

Top left: Locomotive of the Johnson-Pollock Lumber Company northeast of Grass Lake. This little narrow-gauge Shay, built in 1886, is seen here around 1912 on its way to the company sawmill at Jerome on the Southern Pacific line to Klamath Falls.

Left: The Tampa Box Factory, owned by the Northern California Lumber Company. White pine from the Mt. Shasta region was used extensively to produce fruit boxes, crates, and other wooden containers. Miller photo, 1908.

In July 1908, Miller was at work on another major commission, this time for the Northern California Lumber Company based in Hilt, near the Oregon border. This logging operation grew out of an old sawmill on Cottonwood Creek built in 1855. John Hilt acquired the mill in 1877 and improved the operation until 1890. He sold out to a group that called themselves the Hilt Sugar Pine Company. Reorganized in 1907 as the Northern California Lumber Company, the mill produced 35,000 board feet per day, but was losing money. The company had no railroad, and logs were supplied to the sawmill by chutes and ox teams. Saved from financial disaster by a loan from the Fruit Growers Supply Company, which needed a steady supply of wooden fruit boxes, the Company built a box factory and planing mill at Hilt. Simultaneously they constructed ten miles of standard gauge railroad track from timber to the mill on Cottonwood Creek near Hilt and the lumber yard in town. Charles Miller was called in to record the changes, including the Company's Climax locomotives and their operations on leased timberlands south of Hilt at Soda Creek and Sims. The improvements to the operation, and Miller's impressive photograph album, failed to improve the company's financial situation. Northern California Lumber Company slid deeper in debt and, by 1910, the operation was taken over by Fruit Growers Supply Company, which continued logging near Hilt until the great depression dealt the death blow in 1932. Box making at the Hilt plant continued until 1973.

Top left: Officials of the Northern California Lumber Company watch a demonstration of a new compressed air bucking saw. Steam driven saws were quite common after 1900, and were a logical extension of steam power available in the woods from the steam donkeys. Compressed air, however, seems odd since the air compressor would have to be powered in turn by steam from the donkey. Miller photo, 1908.

Left: A Climax engine of the Northern California Lumber Company pulls a lumber train from the mill on Cottonwood Creek, stopping long enough for Charles Miller to take a picture. 1908.

One of the many popular postcards Charles Miller made of Crater Lake. Miller held the exclusive contract to produce souvenir photos of Crater Lake National Park in 1915. His studio in Klamath Falls offered a variety of scenic views, also rodeo and hunting and fishing scenes of the region.

Klamath Falls, Oregon, by Charles Miller, ca.1910. He moved his photographic studio here after the Southern Pacific Railroad reached Klamath Falls in 1909. Miller could make the trip between his studio and Mt. Shasta in a half day by train.

140

ACKNOWLEDGMENTS AND CREDITS:

All photographs, credited on page, were provided through the courtesy of the California State Library, Sacramento, and the Heritage Junction Museum, McCloud. A special thanks to those who helped bring Charles Miller's photographs into the light: Gary F. Kurutz, Curator of Special Collections, California State Library, whose appreciation of the documentary value of Miller's albums encouraged their publication in book form; Norman K. Linn of the Heritage Junction Museum in McCloud, whose rich knowledge of the Museum's photographic collection expanded the scope of the book; Gerald Hoertling and Dennis Berryman, who along with Norman Linn, generously gave of their time and knowledge of logging and railroading, the history of McCloud and the Mt. Shasta region; Dennis Freeman, Director Library Services, College of the Siskiyous Library, Weed, California, and Michael Hendryx, Director, Siskiyou County Museum, Yreka California; and Judith Jassen, Museum Manager, Klamath County Museum, and Nancy Sieverts, Anne Ezell, and Lynn Jeche, Klamath County Museum, and Eric Ziller, Eastman West Postcards, Weed, California.

The following museums and libraries are valuable resources for the study of Charles Miller's photographs and the history of the Mt. Shasta region:

THE CALIFORNIA STATE LIBRARY, located in Sacramento and founded in 1850, possesses one of the oldest and most accessible photographic collections devoted to the Golden State. Its social, cultural, political and economic past is documented through approximately 250,000 photographs of people, places, events and subjects. These are supported by scores of photograph albums, portfolios, illustrated books, prints, and a postcard collection of over 12,000 items. Chronologically, the collection covers the state's past from the Gold Rush to the present, and geographically all fifty-eight counties are represented. Highlights include original mammoth plates, stereographs, and albums by San Francisco's great pioneer photographers including C.E. Watkins, Eadweard Muybridge, and I.W. Taber; the San Francisco Chinatown collection of Louis J. Stellman; Panama-Pacific International Exposition glass-plate negative archive of the Cardinell-Vincent Company; the Los Angeles collections of William Fletcher, Arnold Hylen, William Reagh, and F.W. Martin; and the glass-plate collection of Gladding, McBean & Company.

HERITAGE JUNCTION OF McCLOUD INC., the McCloud Museum and Historical Center, a non-profit organization, was founded in 1981 and housed at 320 Main Street in 1985. Primary among the several interests of the Museum is to gather and preserve the artifacts, documents, and photographs that relate to the "Company Town" that was McCloud, Siskiyou County, California; from its founding in 1896 to 1966 when the town was sold and became public. Other interests of the Museum are the history of the settlement of the area, the development of the lumber industry and its ancillary railroads, within the operating area of the McCloud River Lumber Company, its predecessors and successors. A large collection of photographs by Charles R. Miller document the early sawmill and railroad days.

THE SISKIYOU COUNTY MUSEUM was built in 1950 by the County of Siskiyou to collect, preserve, disseminate, and interpret the history of the area for future generations. An important function of the facility is to provide opportunities for people to explore and learn about the county in interesting and favorable ways. To help accomplish this, the Museum has used its collection to organize exhibits on local Indian populations and their cultures, fur trappers, the military influence of Fort Jones (ca 1852), pioneer settlement, gold mining, Chinese, lumbering and other relevant themes. Period environments and a 2 ½ acre Outdoor Museum help convey the life and times of early residents, and special programs illustrate the historical features unique to the county. A research library with books, manuscripts, biographies, scrapbooks, newspapers and over 22,000 photographs is open throughout the year for those engaging in research.

THE COLLEGE OF THE SISKIYOUS is a community college located in Weed, California on the west slope of Mount Shasta. The College of the Siskiyous Library has developed a unique, comprehensive research collection about Mount Shasta for use by students and faculty as well as researchers, writers, historians, scientists, other libraries and museums, businesses, and the public. Today the Mount Shasta Collection is the largest repository of information and documents about Mount Shasta. The collection consists of thousands of books, articles, manuscripts, photographs, maps, prints, and audiovisual materials about the Mount Shasta volcano and the surrounding region.

THE KLAMATH COUNTY MUSEUM offers the visitor the chance to explore the history, peoples, and scenic wonders of Klamath County, Oregon. The museum complex consists of three buildings each telling a different story. The main museum in downtown Klamath Falls at 1451 Main Street houses an extensive collection of Native American artifacts, relics from Pioneer days, and displays on logging and railroading. It also houses a research library, gift shop, and a complete collection of photographs and negatives of Klamath County and its history. The second museum, the Senator George Baldwin Hotel, built in 1906 and located at 31 Main Street, offers the visitor a step back in time. All the original furnishings and exhibits are displayed in each room exactly as they would have been in the early 1900s. The third facility is the Fort Klamath Museum and Park located on the road to Crater Lake National Park. It highlights the history of Fort Klamath, which was established in 1863.

Windgate Press, P.O. Box 1715, Sausalito, California 94965   www.windgatepress.com

INDEX

Burney Falls, Shasta County, by Miller, ca. 1915.